Do We the Packaging?

What is packaging?	2
Food needs packaging	4
No packaging	8
Plastic packaging	12
New packaging	14
Glossary	16

T0011154

What is packaging?

This is packaging.

This is packaging.

This is packaging too!

3

Food needs packaging

Some food needs packaging.

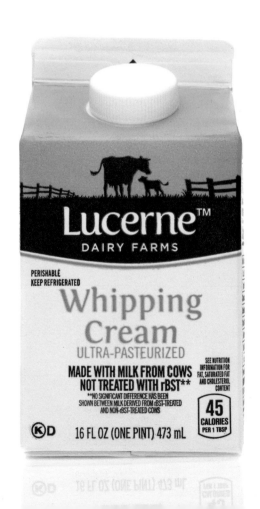

Some food
needs packaging,
to keep it fresh.

Some food
needs packaging,
to keep it safe.

Look at this food.
It needs packaging too.

No packaging

Some food does not need packaging.

The bananas do not need packaging.

The apples do not need packaging.

The oranges do not
need packaging.

Plastic packaging

Some packaging is made from **plastic.** The plastic is not good for the **environment.**

New packaging

Look at this.

This packaging

is made from **card.**

This packaging
is made from cotton.

Glossary

 card

 environment

 plastic